THE OFFICIAL itv SPORT
FORMULAONE
ANNUAL 2011

Written by David Clayton
Designed by Simon Thorley
Dedicated to Jordan Cain

itv STUDIOS

The ITV Sport logo is licensed by ITV Studios Global Entertainment.
All rights reserved.

A Grange Publication

© 2010. Published by Grange Communications Ltd., Edinburgh,
under licence from ITV Studios Global Entertainment. Printed in
the EU.

Photographs © Press Association Images & Thinkstock

ISBN 978-1-907104-81-7

£7.99

CONTENTS

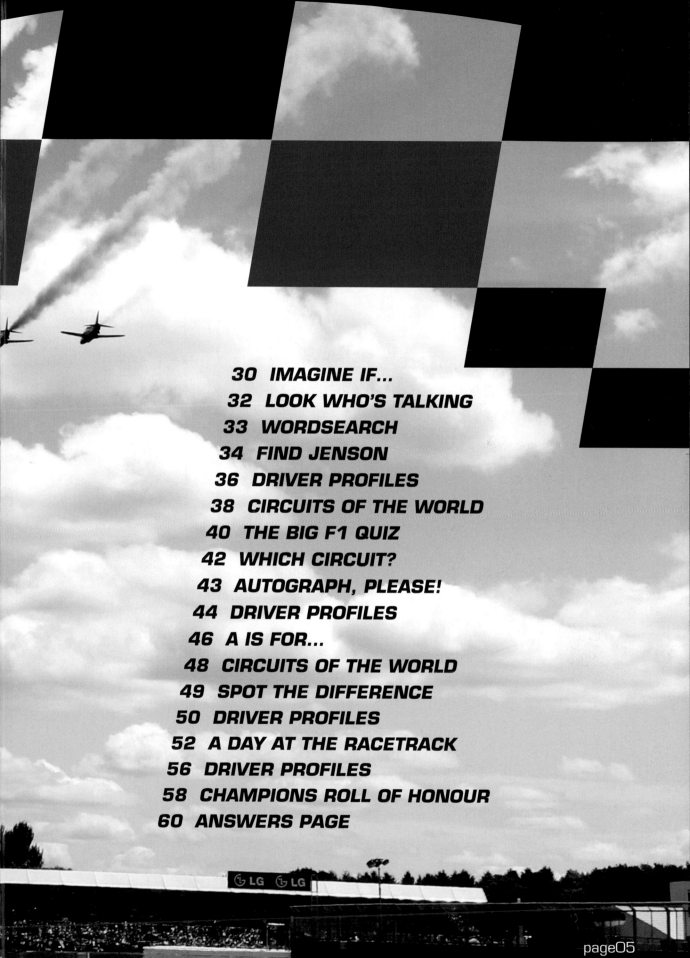

2009 FORMULA ONE SEASON REVIEW

The 17 rounds of the Formula One World Championship began in Australia in March 2009 and ended in Abu Dhabi in November. It was an exciting, controversial and thrilling battle which ultimately saw a new champion crowned.

Suggestions of ways to make the new season more exciting included scrapping the points system and instead giving the championship to the driver with the most wins, but it was decided to leave things the way they were.

The Canadian and French Grands Prix were dropped and the new Abu Dhabi venue was included instead. Brawn GP were the newest team to enter the championship with Honda dropping out. Defending champion Lewis Hamilton was hoping to once again challenge for the title, but he soon discovered that new aerodynamics and tyres had left his team McLaren struggling in the early tests in Barcelona.

Some teams were having trouble adapting to new regulations and by the time they had caught up, the season was half over. Britain's Jenson Button had dreamed of one day winning

the world title, but his efforts had seen him only occasionally threaten to challenge the established leaders.

With a new car and a new team behind him, however, Button's dream was about to come true. Brawn made a stunning start to the 2009 season and Button, who had previously won just one Grand Prix, won six of the first seven races – it was incredible!

The points Button accumulated meant that even with 10 races remaining, if he remained steady and kept picking up points along the way, he would be in with a great chance of winning the title. In fact, the lack of a consistent challenger meant that despite Button failing to win any more races that season and only having two podium finishes in the last 10 races, he still won the championship by 11 points with Sebastian Vettel finishing second.

Lewis Hamilton finished fifth with 49 points – almost half Button's total – and Brawn also picked up the Constructor's Championship in their debut season.

Well done Jenson!

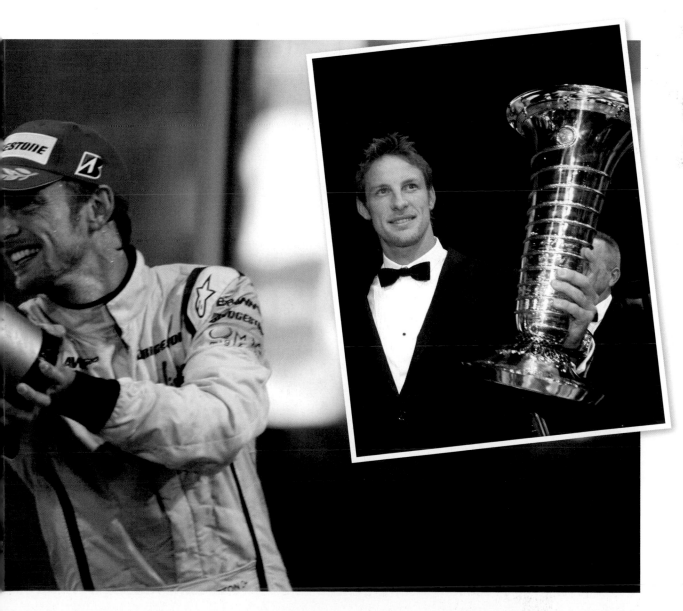

2009 FORMULA ONE SEASON RESULTS

ABU DHABI
YAS MARINA CIRCUIT, SUNDAY, 1 NOVEMBER 2009

Position	Country	Driver	Car no:	Team	Grid	Race time	Points
1	Germany	Sebastian Vettel	15	Red Bull-Renault	2	1:34:03.414	10
2	Australia	Mark Webber	14	Red Bull-Renault	3	1:34:21.271	8
3	Great Britain	Jenson Button	22	Brawn-Mercedes	5	1:34:21.881	6

BRAZIL
INTERLAGOS, SUNDAY, 18 OCTOBER 2009

Position	Country	Driver	Car no:	Team	Grid	Race time	Points
1	Australia	Mark Webber	14	Red Bull-Renault	2	1:32:23.081	10
2	Poland	Robert Kubica	5	BMW Sauber	8	1:32:30.707	8
3	Great Britain	Lewis Hamilton	1	McLaren-Mercedes	17	1:32:42.025	6

JAPAN
SUZUKA, SUNDAY, 4 OCTOBER 2009

Position	Country	Driver	Car no:	Team	Grid	Race time	Points
1	Germany	Sebastian Vettel	15	Red Bull-Renault	1	1:28:20.443	10
2	Italy	Jarno Trulli	9	Toyota	2	1:28:25.243	8
3	Great Britain	Lewis Hamilton	1	McLaren-Mercedes	3	1:28:26.843	6

SINGAPORE
SINGAPORE, SUNDAY, 27 SEPTEMBER 2009

Position	Country	Driver	Car no:	Team	Grid	Race time	Points
1	Great Britain	Lewis Hamilton	1	McLaren-Mercedes	1	1:56:06.337	10
2	Germany	Timo Glock	10	Toyota	6	1:56:18.971	8
3	Spain	Fernando Alonso	7	Renault	5	1:56:22.961	6

ITALY
MONZA, SUNDAY, 13 SEPTEMBER 2009

Position	Country	Driver	Car no:	Team	Grid	Race time	Points
1	Brazil	Rubens Barrichello	23	Brawn-Mercedes	5	1:16:21.706	10
2	Great Britain	Jenson Button	22	Brawn-Mercedes	6	1:16:24.572	8
3	Finland	Kimi Räikkönen	4	Ferrari	3	1:16:52.370	6

BELGIUM
SPA-FRANCORCHAMPS, SUNDAY, 30 AUGUST 2009

Position	Country	Driver	Car no:	Team	Grid	Race time	Points
1	Finland	Kimi Räikkönen	4	Ferrari	6	1:23:50.995	10
2	Italy	Giancarlo Fisichella	21	Force India-Mercedes	1	1:23:51.934	8
3	Germany	Sebastian Vettel	15	Red Bull-Renault	8	1:23:54.870	6

EUROPE
VALENCIA, SUNDAY, 23 AUGUST 2009

Position	Country	Driver	Car no:	Team	Grid	Race time	Points
1	Brazil	Rubens Barrichello	23	Brawn-Mercedes	3	1:35:51.289	10
2	Great Britain	Lewis Hamilton	1	McLaren-Mercedes	1	1:35:53.647	8
3	Finland	Kimi Räikkönen	4	Ferrari	6	1:36:07.283	6

HUNGARY
HUNGARORING, SUNDAY, 26 JULY 2009

Position	Country	Driver	Car no:	Team	Grid	Race time	Points
1	Great Britain	Lewis Hamilton	1	McLaren-Mercedes	4	1:38:23.876	10
2	Finland	Kimi Räikkönen	4	Ferrari	7	1:38:34.881	8
3	Australia	Mark Webber	14	Red Bull-Renault	3	1:30:39.884	6

GERMANY
NÜRBURGRING, SUNDAY, 12 JULY 2009

Position	Country	Driver	Car no:	Team	Grid	Race time	Points
1	Australia	Mark Webber	14	Red Bull-Renault	1	1:36:43.310	10
2	Germany	Sebastian Vettel	15	Red Bull-Renault	4	1:36:52.562	8
3	Brazil	Felipe Massa	3	Ferrari	8	1:36:59.216	6

GREAT BRITAIN
SILVERSTONE, SUNDAY, 21 JUNE 2009

Position	Country	Driver	Car no:	Team	Grid	Race time	Points
1	Germany	Sebastian Vettel	15	Red Bull-Renault	1	1:22:49.328	10
2	Australia	Mark Webber	14	Red Bull-Renault	3	1:23:04.516	8
3	Brazil	Rubens Barrichello	23	Brawn-Mercedes	2	1:23:30.483	6

TURKEY
ISTANBUL, SUNDAY, 7 JUNE 2009

Position	Country	Driver	Car no:	Team	Grid	Race time	Points
1	Great Britain	Jenson Button	22	Brawn-Mercedes	2	1:26:24.848	10
2	Australia	Mark Webber	14	Red Bull-Renault	4	1:26:31.562	8
3	Germany	Sebastian Vettel	15	Red Bull-Renault	1	1:26:32.309	6

MONACO
MONTE CARLO, SUNDAY, 24 MAY 2009

Position	Country	Driver	Car no:	Team	Grid	Race time	Points
1	Great Britain	Jenson Button	22	Brawn-Mercedes	1	1:40:44.282	10
2	Brazil	Rubens Barrichello	23	Brawn-Mercedes	3	1:40:51.948	8
3	Finland	Kimi Räikkönen	4	Ferrari	2	1:40:57.724	6

2009 FORMULA ONE SEASON RESULTS

SPAIN
BARCELONA, SUNDAY, 10 MAY 2009

Position	Country	Driver	Car no:	Team	Grid	Race time	Points
1	Great Britain	Jenson Button	22	Brawn-Mercedes	1	1:37:19.202	10
2	Brazil	Rubens Barrichello	23	Brawn-Mercedes	3	1:37:32.258	8
3	Australia	Mark Webber	14	Red Bull-Renault	5	1:37:33.126	6

BAHRAIN
SAKHIR, SUNDAY, 26 APRIL 2009

Position	Country	Driver	Car no:	Team	Grid	Race time	Points
1	Great Britain	Jenson Button	22	Brawn-Mercedes	4	1:31:48.182	10
2	Germany	Sebastian Vettel	15	Red Bull-Renault	3	1:31:55.369	8
3	Italy	Jarno Trulli	9	Toyota	1	1:31:57.352	6

CHINA
SHANGHAI, SUNDAY, 19 APRIL 2009

Position	Country	Driver	Car no:	Team	Grid	Race time	Points
1	Germany	Sebastian Vettel	15	Red Bull-Renault	1	1:57:43.485	10
2	Australia	Mark Webber	14	Red Bull-Renault	3	1:57:54.455	8
3	Great Britain	Jenson Button	22	Brawn-Mercedes	5	1:58:28.460	6

MALAYSIA
SEPANG, SUNDAY, 5 APRIL 2009

Position	Country	Driver	Car no:	Team	Grid	Race time	Points
1	Great Britain	Jenson Button	22	Brawn-Mercedes	1	0:55:30.622	5
2	Germany	Nick Heidfeld	6	BMW Sauber	10	0:55:53.344	4
3	Germany	Timo Glock	10	Toyota	3	0:55:54.135	3

AUSTRALIA
ALBERT PARK, SUNDAY, 29 MARCH 2009

Position	Country	Driver	Car no:	Team	Grid	Race time	Points
1	Great Britain	Jenson Button	22	Brawn-Mercedes	1	1:34:15.784	10
2	Brazil	Rubens Barrichello	23	Brawn-Mercedes	2	1:34:16.591	8
3	Italy	Jarno Trulli	9	Toyota	19	1:34:17.384	6

2009 FORMULA ONE SEASON RESULTS

F1 DRIVERS' CHAMPIONSHIP FINAL STANDINGS 2009

	Driver	Team	Points
1	Jenson Button	Brawn-Mercedes	95
2	Sebastian Vettel	Red Bull-Renault	84
3	Rubens Barrichello	Brawn-Mercedes	77
4	Mark Webber	Red Bull-Renault	69.5
5	Lewis Hamilton	McLaren-Mercedes	49
6	Kimi Räikkönen	Ferrari	48
7	Nico Rosberg	Williams-Toyota	34.5
8	Jarno Trulli	Toyota	32.5
9	Fernando Alonso	Renault	26
10	Timo Glock	Toyota	24
11	Felipe Massa	Ferrari	22
12	Heikki Kovalainen	McLaren-Mercedes	22
13	Nick Heidfeld	BMW Sauber	19
14	Robert Kubica	BMW Sauber	17
15	Giancarlo Fisichella	Ferrari	8
16	Sébastien Buemi	STR-Ferrari	6
17	Adrian Sutil	Force India-Mercedes	5
18	Kamui Kobayashi	Toyota	3
19	Sébastien Bourdais	STR-Ferrari	2
=20	Romain Grosjean	Renault	0
=20	Vitantonio Liuzzi	Force India-Mercedes	0
=20	Jaime Alguersuari	STR-Ferrari	0
=20	Kazuki Nakajima	Williams-Toyota	0
=20	Luca Badoer	Ferrari	0
=20	Nelson Piquet Jnr	Renault	0

CONSTRUCTORS' CHAMPIONSHIP

	Driver	Points
1	Brawn-Mercedes	172
2	Red Bull-Renault	153.5
3	McLaren-Mercedes	71
4	Ferrari	70
5	Toyota	59.5
6	BMW Sauber	36
7	Williams-Toyota	34.5
8	Renault	26
9	Force India-Mercedes	13
10	STR-Ferrari	8

ABU DHABI GRAND PRIX
YAS MARINA CIRCUIT, YAS ISLAND, ABU DHABI

FIRST RACE: 2009
CIRCUIT LENGTH: 5.522 KM
LAPS: 55
BUILT: 2009
CAPACITY: 41,093

AUSTRALIAN GRAND PRIX
ALBERT PARK, MELBOURNE

FIRST RACE: 1996
CIRCUIT LENGTH: 5.272 KM
LAPS: 58
BUILT: 1996
CAPACITY: 80,000
RECORD CROWD: 300,000 (OVER 4 DAYS)

BAHRAIN GRAND PRIX
BAHRAIN INTERNATIONAL RACING CIRCUIT, SAKHIR

FIRST RACE: 2004
CIRCUIT LENGTH: 5.381 KM
LAPS: 57
BUILT: 2003/2004
CAPACITY: 50,000
RECORD CROWD: 24,000 (IN 2008)

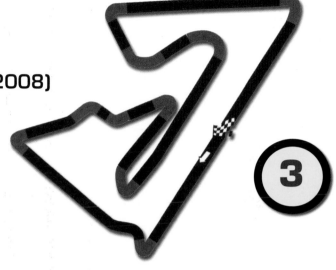

3

BELGIAN GRAND PRIX
SPA FRANCORCHAMPS CIRCUIT, FRANCORCHAMPS

FIRST RACE: 1983 (REVISED SHORTER VERSION)
CIRCUIT LENGTH: 6.963 KM
LAPS: 44
BUILT: 1924 (STREET CIRCUIT)
CAPACITY: APPROX 90,000 (STREET CIRCUIT)
RECORD CROWD: 150,000 (OVER 3 DAYS)

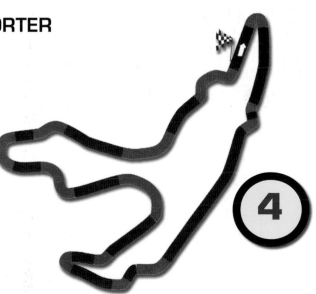

4

JAIME ALGUERSUARI

TEAM: *TORO ROSSO*
BORN: *23/03/1990*
NATIONALITY: *SPANISH*
BIRTHPLACE: *BARCELONA, SPAIN*
WORLD CHAMPIONSHIPS: *0*
HIGHEST FINISH: *9*
RACE WINS: *0*
TOTAL POINTS: *3*

FERNANDO ALONSO

TEAM: *FERRARI*
BORN: *29/07/1981*
NATIONALITY: *SPANISH*
BIRTHPLACE: *OVIEDO, SPAIN*
WORLD CHAMPIONSHIPS: *2*
HIGHEST FINISH: *1*
RACE WINS: *23*
TOTAL POINTS: *700*

RUBENS BARRICHELLO

TEAM: *WILLIAMS*
BORN: *23/05/1972*
NATIONALITY: *BRAZILIAN*
BIRTHPLACE: *SAO PAULO, BRAZIL*
WORLD CHAMPIONSHIPS: *0*
HIGHEST FINISH: *1*
RACE WINS: *11*
TOTAL POINTS: *636*

SÉBASTIEN BUEMI

TEAM: *TORO ROSSO*
BORN: *31/10/1988*
NATIONALITY: *SWISS*
BIRTHPLACE: *AIGLE, SWITZERLAND*
WORLD CHAMPIONSHIPS: *0*
HIGHEST FINISH: *7*
RACE WINS: *0*
TOTAL POINTS: *13*

SPOT THE DIFFERENCE

PICTURE A AND B ARE THE SAME – OR ARE THEY? CAN YOU SPOT AND CIRCLE THE SIX DIFFERENCES IN PICTURE B?

BRAZILIAN GRAND PRIX
AUTODROMO JOSE CARLOS PACE, SAO PAULO

FIRST RACE: 1973
CIRCUIT LENGTH: 4.283 KM
LAPS: 71
BUILT: 1940
CAPACITY: 80,000

5

BRITISH GRAND PRIX
SILVERSTONE CIRCUIT, NORTHANTS

FIRST RACE: 1950
CIRCUIT LENGTH: 5.110 KM
LAPS: 60
BUILT: 1948
CAPACITY: 90,000
RECORD CROWD: 310,000
(OVER 3 DAYS) IN 2009

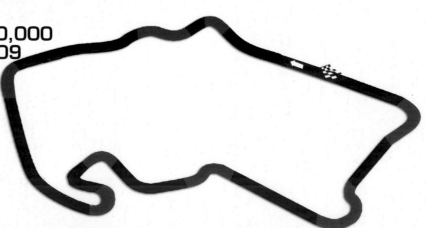

6

CANADIAN GRAND PRIX
CIRCUIT GILLES VILLENEUVE, MONTREAL

FIRST RACE: 1978
CIRCUIT LENGTH: 4.336 KM
LAPS: 70
BUILT: 1978
CAPACITY: 100,000
RECORD CROWD: 100,000

CHINESE GRAND PRIX
SHANGHAI CIRCUIT, SHANGHAI

FIRST RACE: 2004
CIRCUIT LENGTH: 5.419 KM
LAPS: 56
BUILT: 2003/2004
CAPACITY: 200,000

GUESS WHO?

HERE ARE FOUR IMAGES OF SOME CURRENT F1 STARS, CAN YOU GUESS WHO THEY ARE?

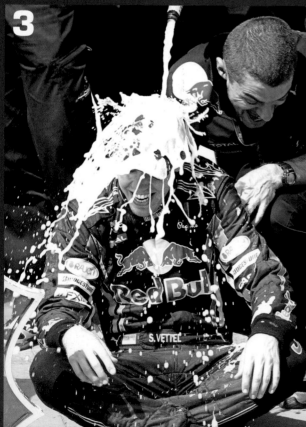

Answers on page 60/61

JENSON BUTTON

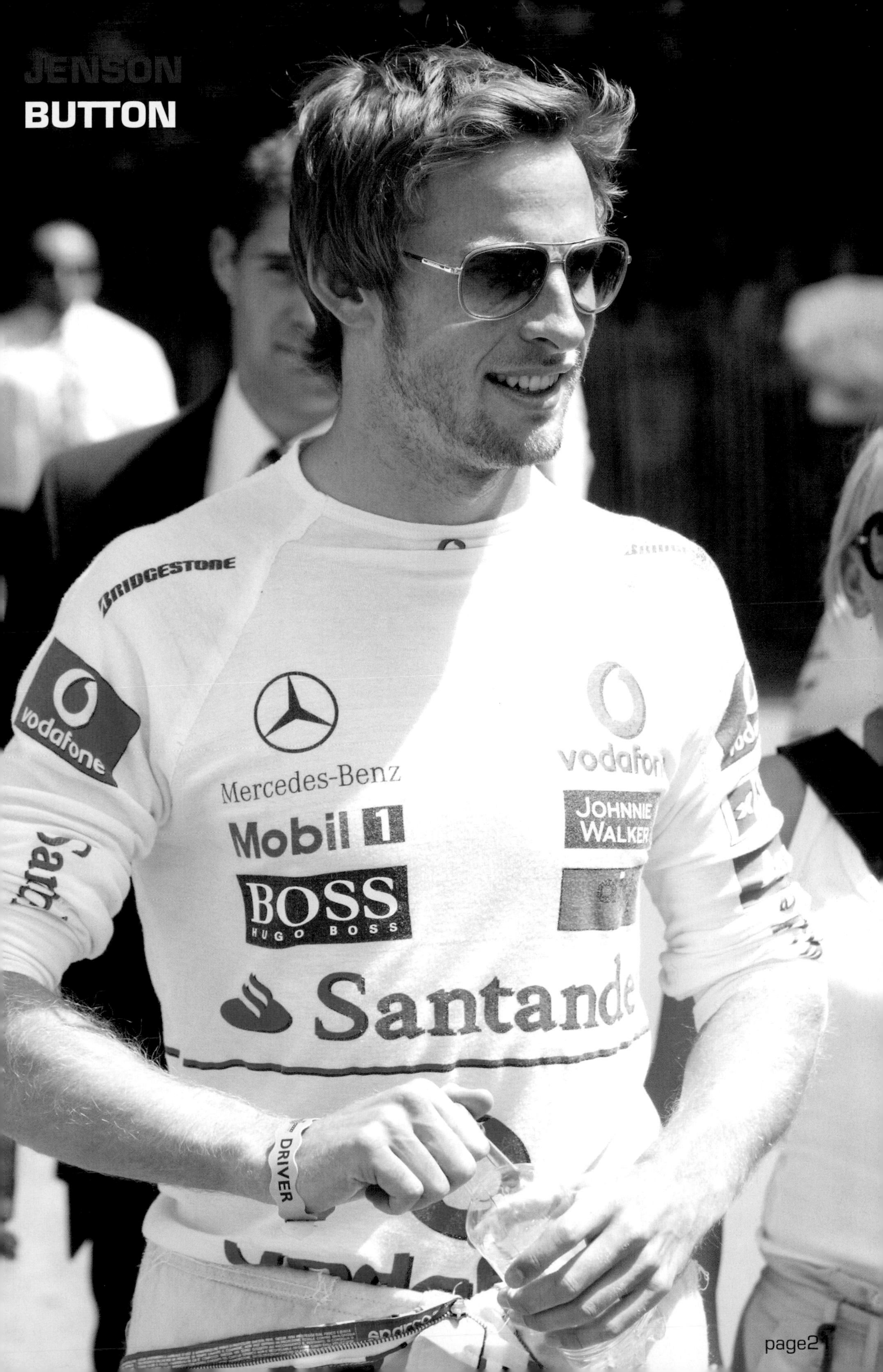

JENSON BUTTON

TEAM: MCLAREN
BORN: 19/01/1980
NATIONALITY: BRITISH
BIRTHPLACE: FROME, UK
WORLD CHAMPIONSHIPS: 1
HIGHEST FINISH: 1
RACE WINS: 9
TOTAL POINTS: 470

KARUN CHANDHOK

TEAM: HRT
BORN: 19/01/1984
NATIONALITY: INDIAN
BIRTHPLACE: CHENNAI, INDIA
WORLD CHAMPIONSHIPS: 0
HIGHEST FINISH: 14
RACE WINS: 0
TOTAL POINTS: 0

TIMO GLOCK

TEAM: VIRGIN
BORN: 18/03/1982
NATIONALITY: GERMAN
BIRTHPLACE: LINDENFELS, GERMANY
WORLD CHAMPIONSHIPS: 0
HIGHEST FINISH: 2
RACE WINS: 0
TOTAL POINTS: 51

LUCAS DI GRASSI

TEAM: VIRGIN
BORN: 11/08/1984
NATIONALITY: BRAZILIAN
BIRTHPLACE: SAO PAULO, BRAZIL
WORLD CHAMPIONSHIPS: 0
HIGHEST FINISH: 14
RACE WINS: 0
TOTAL POINTS: 0

DETAILS CORRECT TO 31/07/10

DESIGN YOUR OWN F1 CAR

WE'VE STRIPPED
AN F1 CAR OF ITS
DESIGN SO YOU
CAN PUT YOUR
OWN COLOURS
ON – THE MORE
STRIKING THE
BETTER!

F1 CROSSWORD

READ THE CLUES AND PUT THE ANSWERS INTO THE CROSSWORD PUZZLE. SEE IF YOU CAN FILL EVERY BLANK IN THE BOX!

ACROSS

1 German driver now with Virgin (4,5)
2 Where every driver wants to start the race from (4,8)
6 This is held in front of a driver during a pit-stop - though he can't eat it! (8)
8 Electric blanket that is wrapped around the wheels prior to races (4,6)
9 Nationality of Jarno Trulli (7)
11 High ranking official employed at a Grand Prix to make important decisions (7)
12 Tight sequence of corners with alternate directions (7)
14 Race marshals will wave this if there is danger on the track (6,4)
17 A drink the winning drivers often spray on those who finish second and third (9)
18 Drivers prefer these when it rains (3,5)

DOWN

1 What the winning driver is awarded (3,6)
3 Location of British Grand Prix (11)
4 Indian driver who drives for HRT (5,8)
5 Vitantonio Liuzzi drives for this team (5,5)
7 Area drivers must head for if given a drive through penalty (3,4)
10 The slowest car on the track that is often seen out in front! (6,3)
12 Where the driver sits (7)
13 A top three finish will ensure a place on this (6)
15 Country Robert Kubica was born in (6)
16 Every driver must wear one of these (6)

Solution on page 60/61

KNOW YOUR FLAGS!

MANY TRACKSIDE FLAGS CAN BE SEEN WAVING DURING A RACE – BUT DO YOU KNOW WHAT THEY ARE FOR? HERE IS OUR GUIDE TO F1 FLAGS SO THAT THE NEXT TIME YOU'RE WATCHING A RACE, YOU'LL KNOW EXACTLY WHAT THEY MEAN AND WHY THEY ARE BEING WAVED....

CHEQUERED FLAG

This is the most distinctive and famous of all the Grand Prix flags. When you see this being waved it indicates to drivers that the session has ended. It is shown first to the winner and then to every car that crosses the line behind him and means 'race over'!

YELLOW FLAG

Yellow, in this case, means danger. It could be a stranded car ahead or some other potential problem for drivers. A single waved yellow flag warns drivers to slow down, while two waved yellow flags at the same post means that drivers must slow down and be prepared to stop if necessary. Overtaking at this point is prohibited for obvious reasons.

GREEN FLAG

The green flag is a positive for drivers – it basically means 'all clear'. The driver has now passed the potential danger point and restrictions imposed by yellow flags have been lifted.

RED FLAG

If the red flag is waved, it is usually because the session has been stopped, usually due to an accident or poor track conditions. Either way, it's time to stop!

BLUE FLAG

It may mean a clean beach if you are by the seaside, but at an F1 race, the blue flag is waved to warn a driver that he is about to be lapped and to let the faster car overtake. Pass three blue flags without complying and drivers risks being penalised. Blue lights are also displayed at the end of the pit lane when the pit exit is open and a car on track is approaching – handy to know given the speed cars reach during the race.

YELLOW AND RED STRIPED FLAG

This warns drivers of a slippery track surface, usually due to oil or water.

BLACK WITH ORANGE CIRCLE FLAG

Accompanied by a car number, it warns a driver that he has a mechanical problem and must return to his pit – if you see this flag being waved at you, your number is literally up!

HALF BLACK, HALF WHITE FLAG

Not a popular flag for drivers to see when accompanied by their car number because it means the stewards believe they've been guilty of unsporting behaviour. If the warning is heeded, it may be followed by a black flag...

BLACK FLAG

Again, as you might imagine given the colour, when accompanied by a car number, it directs a driver to return to his pit and is most often used to signal to the driver that he has been excluded from the race. Not a good flag to see!

WHITE FLAG

This is not a sign of surrender – just a warning that a slow moving vehicle is on the track.

F1WORLDCIRCUITS

EUROPEAN GRAND PRIX (SPAIN)
STREET CIRCUIT, VALENCIA

FIRST RACE: 2008
CIRCUIT LENGTH: 5.387 KM
LAPS: 57
BUILT: 2008 (STREET CIRCUIT)
CAPACITY: 112,771

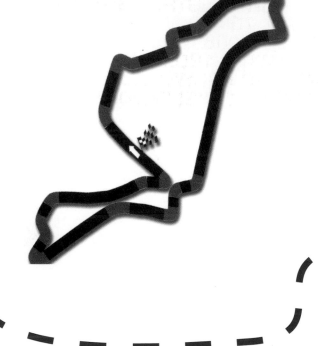

9

GERMAN GRAND PRIX
HOCKENHEIMRING, HOCKENHEIM

FIRST RACE: 2002 (AS A NEW TRACK)
CIRCUIT LENGTH: 4.547 KM
LAPS: 67
BUILT: 2002
CAPACITY: 120,000

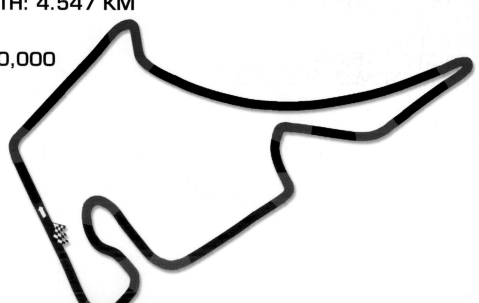

10

HUNGARIAN GRAND PRIX
HUNGARORING CIRCUIT, BUDAPEST

FIRST RACE: 1986
CIRCUIT LENGTH: 4.355 KM
LAPS: 70
BUILT: 1986
CAPACITY: 120,000
RECORD CROWD: 200,000
(OVER 3 DAYS) IN 2008

11

ITALIAN GRAND PRIX
MONZA CIRCUIT, MONZA

FIRST RACE: 1950
CIRCUIT LENGTH: 5.760 KM
LAPS: 53
BUILT: 1950
CAPACITY: 115,000
RECORD CROWD: 100,000

12

IMAGINE IF...

FERNANDO ALONSO DROVE ANY OF THESE OLD BANGERS...

HE'S ONE OF THE GREATEST F1 DRIVERS IN THE WORLD, BUT HOW WOULD HE PERFORM IF HE WAS FORCED TO DRIVE SOME OF THESE ALTERNATIVE MODES OF TRANSPORT...

THE THREE WHEELER

NODDY CAR

THE BATMOBILE

F1 UNPLUGGED

FERNANDO THE FASTEST
MILKMAN IN THE WEST

MUNSTER TRUCKS

LOOK WHO'S TALKING

WE DON'T KNOW FOR SURE WHAT THE DRIVERS WERE SAYING AT THE TIME THESE PICTURES WERE TAKEN – BUT WE CAN MAKE A PRETTY GOOD GUESS!

F1WORDSEARCH

CAN YOU SPOT 10 F1 DRIVERS IN THE WORDSEARCH BELOW? REMEMBER, THE NAMES COULD BE IN ANY DIRECTION.

```
M Q X K K L N P N Z D B F C M
G R E B S O R O C I N E M N K
V R J M F R M Z Y K L V O Y C
I L E W I S H A M I L T O N O
T K L L T L K B P L T N L N L
A R R N B T L E Q U D R N I G
L E H H T R M U B R N K T B O
Y B K T M A U N R L Z U Y M M
P B M X S L O N G T S L N M I
E E Q S P S G N O N O L V T T
T W A H N C R N A S L N R R C
R K L E W Q P I D M E N R J N
O R J T L H R M W G G N T A X
V A D W Q D M G L D H R N G J
N M J M A R F V N L H H Q A M
```

FORZA
FERRARI
LA PLATA
ARGENTINA

Answers on page 60/61

LEWIS HAMILTON

TEAM: MCLAREN
BORN: 07/01/1985
NATIONALITY: BRITISH
BIRTHPLACE: STEVENAGE, UK
WORLD CHAMPIONSHIPS: 1
HIGHEST FINISH: 1
RACE WINS: 13
TOTAL POINTS: 413

NICO HULKENBERG

TEAM: WILLIAMS
BORN: 19/08/1987
NATIONALITY: GERMAN
BIRTHPLACE: EMMERICH, GERMANY
WORLD CHAMPIONSHIPS: 0
HIGHEST FINISH: 10
RACE WINS: 0
TOTAL POINTS: 2

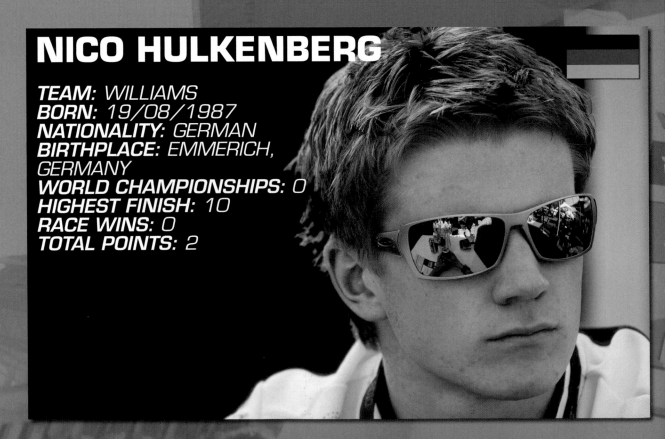

KAMUI KOBAYASHI

TEAM: *BMW SAUBER*
BORN: *13/09/1986*
NATIONALITY: *JAPANESE*
BIRTHPLACE: *AMAGASAKI, JAPAN*
WORLD CHAMPIONSHIPS: *0*
HIGHEST FINISH: *6*
RACE WINS: *0*
TOTAL POINTS: *18*

HEIKKI KOVALAINEN

TEAM: *LOTUS*
BORN: *19/10/1981*
NATIONALITY: *FINNISH*
BIRTHPLACE: *SUOMUSSALMI, FINLAND*
WORLD CHAMPIONSHIPS: *0*
HIGHEST FINISH: *1*
RACE WINS: *1*
TOTAL POINTS: *105*

JAPANESE GRAND PRIX
SUZUKA, MIE PREFECTURE, JAPAN

FIRST RACE: 1962
CIRCUIT LENGTH: 5.773 KM
LAPS: 53
BUILT: 1962
CAPACITY: 100,000
RECORD CROWD: 100,000

13

MALAYSIAN GRAND PRIX
SEPANG INTERNATIONAL CIRCUIT, KUALA LUMPUR

FIRST RACE: 1999
CIRCUIT LENGTH: 5.510 KM
LAPS: 56
BUILT: 1998
CAPACITY: 130,000
RECORD CROWD: 115,794

14

MONACO GRAND PRIX
CIRCUIT DE MONACO, MONTE CARLO

FIRST RACE: 1950
CIRCUIT LENGTH: 3.320 KM
LAPS: 78
BUILT: 1950 (STREET CIRCUIT)
CAPACITY: 50,000

15

SINGAPORE
MARINA BAY, SINGAPORE

FIRST RACE: 2008
CIRCUIT LENGTH: 5.037 KM
LAPS: 61
BUILT: 2008 (STREET CIRCUIT)
CAPACITY: 100,000
RECORD CROWD:
100,000 IN 2008

16

THE BIG F1 QUIZ

1, WHO IS THIS?

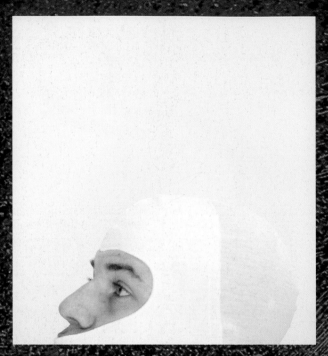

2, WHICH DRIVER HAS JUST WON A GRAND PRIX IN THIS PICTURE?

3, NAME FIVE GERMAN F1 DRIVERS.

4, WHAT IS THIS GUY'S JOB TITLE?

5, WHICH TEAM DID JENSON BUTTON WIN THE 2009 DRIVERS' CHAMPIONSHIP WITH?

6, WHICH COUNTRY IS VITALY PETROV FROM?

7, HOW MANY CHAMPIONSHIPS HAS MICHAEL SCHUMACHER WON?

8, WHICH TWO GRAND PRIX CIRCUITS WERE DROPPED IN 2009?

9, WHERE IS THIS?

10, CAN YOU WORK OUT WHO THIS IS?

16, WHERE DID LEWIS HAMILTON FINISH IN THE 2010 BRITISH GRAND PRIX?

17, HOW MANY WORLD CHAMPIONSHIPS HAS FERNANDO ALONSO WON?

18, WHICH F1 TEAM DO YOU ASSOCIATE THIS IMAGE WITH?

11, WHAT DO THE SINGAPORE AND MONACO GRAND PRIX HAVE IN COMMON?

12, WHO SUFFERED A NASTY EYE INJURY DURING THE 2009 SEASON, THREATENING HIS CAREER?

13, WHAT WAS SO SPECIAL ABOUT THE 2009 F1 SEASON?

14, WHO'S NAME IS THIS AN ANAGRAM OF – SON RICE BOG?

15, WHO IS THIS?

19, CAN YOU IDENTIFY THIS F1 DRIVER?

20, THOUGH HE RETURNED FOR THE 2010 SEASON, WHICH YEAR DID MICHAEL SCHUMACHER ORIGINALLY RETIRE?
A) 2005 B) 2006 C) 2007

WHICHCIRCUIT?

YOU'D HAVE TO BE AN F1 EXPERT TO GET ALL THESE RIGHT – SEE IF YOU CAN WORK OUT AT WHICH CIRCUITS THE IMAGES BELOW WERE TAKEN...

A

B

C

D

Answers on page 60/61

AUTOGRAPHPLEASE!

EVER WONDERED HOW YOUR FAVOURITE DRIVER SIGNS HIS NAME?
BELOW, WE'VE MANAGED TO COLLECT A FEW AUTOGRAPHS TO
FIND OUT WHO HAS STYLE AND WHO JUST SCRIBBLES!

SCHUMACHER

WEBBER

BUTTON

MASSA

HAMILTON

ALONSO

TRULLI

ROBERT KUBICA

TEAM: RENAULT
BORN: 07/12/1984
NATIONALITY: POLISH
BIRTHPLACE: KRAKOW, POLAND
WORLD CHAMPIONSHIPS: 0
HIGHEST FINISH: 1
RACE WINS: 1
TOTAL POINTS: 226

VITANTONIO LIUZZI

TEAM: FORCE INDIA
BORN: 06/08/1981
NATIONALITY: ITALIAN
BIRTHPLACE: LOCOROTONDO, ITALY
WORLD CHAMPIONSHIPS: 0
HIGHEST FINISH: 6
RACE WINS: 0
TOTAL POINTS: 17

FELIPE MASSA

TEAM: FERRARI
BORN: 25/04/1981
NATIONALITY: BRAZILIAN
BIRTHPLACE: SAO PAULO, BRAZIL
WORLD CHAMPIONSHIPS: 0
HIGHEST FINISH:
RACE WINS: 11
TOTAL POINTS: 405

VITALY PETROV

TEAM: RENAULT
BORN: 08/09/1984
NATIONALITY: RUSSIAN
BIRTHPLACE: VYBORG, RUSSIA
WORLD CHAMPIONSHIPS: 0
HIGHEST FINISH: 7
RACE WINS: 0
TOTAL POINTS: 7

DETAILS CORRECT TO 31/07/10

A IS FOR...

A IS FOR AERODYNAMICS

This is the study of airflow over and around an object and is a vital area that influences Formula One car design.

B IS FOR BALLAST

These are the weights that are fixed around the car to maximise its balance and bring it up to the minimum weight limit – a bit like a jockey riding a horse or a boxer at a weigh-in. It has to be fair to all so similar weights are needed.

C IS FOR CHASSIS

This is the main part of a racing car which the engine and suspension are attached on to.

D IS FOR DIFFUSER

You will find the diffuser at the rear section of the car's floor where the air flowing under the car exits. The design of the diffuser is vital to an F1 racing car as it controls the speed at which the air exits – the faster its exit, the lower the air pressure beneath the car, and hence the more down force the car can generate. In simple terms it helps the car go faster.

E IS FOR ELECTRONIC FUEL INJECTION

This is a system that injects fuel into the engine and includes an electronic control unit that times and measures the flow. Fuel is delivered in intermittent pulses by the opening and closing of special fuel injectors.

F IS FOR FORMATION LAP

This is the lap before the start of the race when the cars are driven round from the grid to assemble on the grid again ready for the start of the race. It is also sometimes referred to as the warm-up lap or parade lap.

G IS FOR G-FORCE

A word often associated with F1 racing, G-force is a physical force equivalent to one unit of gravity that is multiplied during rapid changes of direction or velocity – but you knew that already! Drivers can experience severe G-force as they take a corner quickly, accelerate or brake.

H IS FOR HARD TYRES

A different compound to soft tyres – they last longer but have less grip.

I IS FOR INSTALLATION LAP

This is a lap (almost) completed on arrival at a circuit where a driver will test vital functions such as throttle, brakes and steering before heading back to the pits - without crossing the finish line.

J IS FOR JUMP START

This term describes when a driver has moved off his grid position before the five red lights have been switched off to signal the start. Sensors detect premature movement and a jump start earns a driver a penalty – not a good way to begin!

K IS FOR KERS

KERS stands for Kinetic Energy Recovery Systems – these were made legal in 2009. KERS recover waste kinetic energy from the car during braking, store that energy and then make it available to propel the car – quite clever, really. The driver has access to the additional power for limited periods per lap, via a 'boost button' on the steering wheel – a bit like having a computer game controller on hand to give the car that extra va-va-voom!

L IS FOR LOLLIPOP

This is the sign on a stick held in front of the car during a pit stop to tell the driver to apply the brakes and then to engage first gear prior to the car being lowered from its jacks – handy for the pit crew who have just a fraction of a second to get out of the way.

M IS FOR MARSHAL

This is the guy who ensures the race is run safely. Marshals have many roles to fill, including observing the spectators to ensure they do not endanger themselves or the drivers, acting as fire wardens, helping to remove stranded cars or drivers from the track and using flags to signal the condition of the track to drivers – rarely a job that passes without incident but an interesting one all the same.

N IS FOR NUMBER PLATE

In 2008, a man paid just over £400,000 for the car registration plate 'F1'!

O IS FOR OVERSTEER

Oversteer is when the back end of a car attempts to spin round during a fast corner. To correct the problem, the driver needs to opposite-lock, meaning turning the front wheels into the skid.

P IS FOR PADDOCK

This is an enclosed area behind the pits in which the teams keep their transporters and motor homes. There is no admission to the public, though a few VIPs seem to get in there from time to time!

Q IS FOR QUALIFYING

This is the knock-out session held on a Saturday during which the drivers compete to set the best time they can in order to determine the starting grid for the race. Needless to say, the fastest gets the pole, the slowest starts at the rear.

R IS FOR RIDE-HEIGHT

This is the height between the track's surface and the floor of the car – it has to be at the legal distance for safety reasons.

S IS FOR SHAKEDOWN

It may sound as though it's straight out of an American police movie, but shakedown in F1 is a short test when a team is trying a different car part for the first time before going back out to drive at 100 percent to set a fast time – it basically checks all is working correctly before the driver goes hell-for-leather!

T IS FOR TEAR-OFF STRIPS

These are the see-through plastic strips that drivers fit to their helmet's visor before the start of the race and then remove as they become dirty – clear vision is crucial when travelling at the speed these guys do.

U IS FOR UNDERTRAY

This is a separate floor to the car that is bolted onto the underside of the monocoque – bet you wish we'd included monocoque in the A to Z now! That's one you can find out for yourselves!

V IS FOR VISCOUS

This is a description of a fluid property related to F1 cars meaning thick or sticky.

W IS FOR WINDSCREEN

Like a normal car in that an F1 car's windscreen is there to protect a driver from wind, rain and flying debris.

X IS FOR X-RAY

Often needed for drivers involved in high speed bumps or crashes!

Y IS FOR YAMAHA

Brilliant in many aspects of motor racing, the Japanese constructers found building successful F1 racing cars hard going and never enjoyed a race winner despite numerous attempts.

Z IS FOR ZOOM LENS

Thousands of high quality photographs are taken during a Grand Prix – close up pictures are taken with expensive zoom lenses.

F1WORLDCIRCUITS

SOUTH KOREAN GRAND PRIX
KOREAN INTERNATIONAL CIRCUIT

17

FIRST RACE: 2010
CIRCUIT LENGTH: 5.621 KM
LAPS: 55
BUILT: 2010
CAPACITY: 135,000
RECORD CROWDS: N/A

SPANISH GRAND PRIX
CIRCUIT DE CATALUNYA, BARCELONA

18

FIRST RACE: 1991
CIRCUIT LENGTH: 4.627 KM
LAPS: 66
LAPS: 50
BUILT: 1991
CAPACITY: 67,730
RECORD CROWD: 2003

TURKISH GRAND PRIX
ISTANBUL PARK CIRCUIT, ISTANBUL
FIRST RACE: 2005

19

CIRCUIT LENGTH: 5.34 KM
LAPS: 58
BUILT: 2005
CAPACITY: 155,000
RECORD CROWD: 40,000

SPOT THE DIFFERENCE

PICTURE A AND B ARE THE SAME – OR ARE THEY? CAN YOU SPOT AND CIRCLE THE SIX DIFFERENCES IN PICTURE B?

PEDRO
DE LA ROSA

TEAM: BMW SAUBER
BORN: 24/02/1971
NATIONALITY: SPANISH
BIRTHPLACE: BARCELONA, SPAIN
WORLD CHAMPIONSHIPS: 0
HIGHEST FINISH: 2
RACE WINS: 0
TOTAL POINTS: 29

NICO
ROSBERG

TEAM: MERCEDES GP
BORN: 27/06/1985
NATIONALITY: GERMAN
BIRTHPLACE: WIESBADEN, GERMANY
WORLD CHAMPIONSHIPS: 0
HIGHEST FINISH: 2
RACE WINS: 0
TOTAL POINTS: 169.5

MICHAEL SCHUMACHER

TEAM: MERCEDES GP
BORN: 03/01/1969
NATIONALITY: GERMAN
BIRTHPLACE: HÜRTH-HERMÜLHEIM, GERMANY
WORLD CHAMPIONSHIPS: 7
HIGHEST FINISH: 1
RACE WINS: 91
TOTAL POINTS: 1407

BRUNO SENNA

TEAM: HRT
BORN: 15/10/1983
NATIONALITY: BRAZILIAN
BIRTHPLACE: SAO PAULO, BRAZIL
WORLD CHAMPIONSHIPS: 0
HIGHEST FINISH: 16
RACE WINS: 0
TOTAL POINTS: 0

ADAYATTHERACETRACK
THE 2010 BRITISH GRAND PRIX

IT'S ONE OF THE MOST EXCITING DATES ON THE SPORTING CALENDAR – THE BRITISH GRAND PRIX. THERE WAS ADDED EXCITEMENT FOR THE 2010 RACE WITH TWO BRITISH DRIVERS AT

THE TOP OF THE DRIVERS' CHAMPIONSHIP – LEWIS HAMILTON AND JENSON BUTTON – AND HUNDREDS OF THOUSANDS OF PEOPLE CAME TO WATCH OVER A SUN-BAKED WEEKEND.

ADAYATTHERACETRACK
THE 2010 BRITISH GRAND PRIX

IT DIDN'T QUITE GO ACCORDING TO PLAN WITH AUSSIE MARK
WEBBER WINNING, BUT AT LEAST LEWIS MANAGED SECOND
PLACE ON THE PODIUM. WE'VE CHOSEN PICTURES TO SHOW

WHAT MAKES SILVERSTONE SUCH A SPECIAL DAY FOR THE DRIVERS AND THE RACE FANS WHO FLOCK TO IT. WHO KNOWS, MAYBE YOU'LL BE ONE OF THEM IN 2011!

ADRIAN SUTIL

TEAM: *FORCE INDIA*
BORN: *11/01/1983*
NATIONALITY: *GERMAN*
BIRTHPLACE: *STARNBERG, GERMANY*
WORLD CHAMPIONSHIPS: *0*
HIGHEST FINISH: *4*
RACE WINS: *0*
TOTAL POINTS: *41*

JARNO TRULLI

TEAM: *LOTUS*
BORN: *13/07/1974*
NATIONALITY: *ITALIAN*
BIRTHPLACE: *PESCARA, ITALY*
WORLD CHAMPIONSHIPS: *0*
HIGHEST FINISH: *1*
RACE WINS: *1*
TOTAL POINTS: *246.5*

SEBASTIAN VETTEL

TEAM: *RED BULL RACING*
BORN: *03/07/1987*
NATIONALITY: *GERMAN*
BIRTHPLACE: *HEPPENHEIM, GERMANY*
WORLD CHAMPIONSHIPS: *0*
HIGHEST FINISH: *1*
RACE WINS: *7*
TOTAL POINTS: *261*

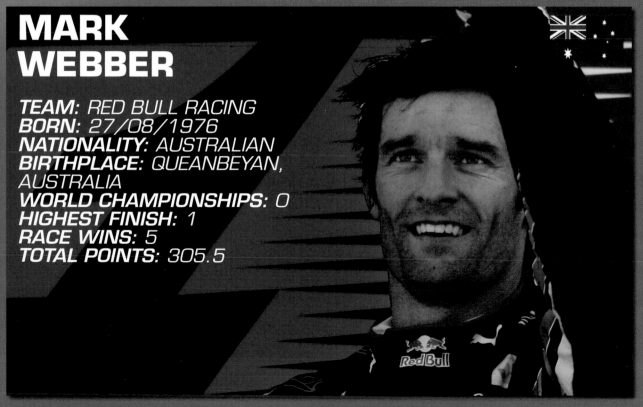

MARK WEBBER

TEAM: *RED BULL RACING*
BORN: *27/08/1976*
NATIONALITY: *AUSTRALIAN*
BIRTHPLACE: *QUEANBEYAN, AUSTRALIA*
WORLD CHAMPIONSHIPS: *0*
HIGHEST FINISH: *1*
RACE WINS: *5*
TOTAL POINTS: *305.5*

DETAILS CORRECT TO 31/07/10

CHAMPIONS ROLL OF HONOUR

HERE IS A LIST OF THE CHAMPION DRIVERS WHO, OVER THE COURSE OF THE F1 SEASON, PROVED THEY WERE THE BEST...

YEAR	CHAMPIONS	CONSTRUCTORS
2009	Jenson BUTTON (GBR)	Brawn-Mercedes
2008	Lewis HAMILTON (GBR)	Mercedes
2007	Kimi RAIKKONEN (FIN)	Ferrari
2006	Fernando ALONSO (SPA)	Renault
2005	Fernando ALONSO (SPA)	Renault
2004	Michael SCHUMACHER (GER)	Ferrari
2003	Michael SCHUMACHER (GER)	Ferrari
2002	Michael SCHUMACHER (GER)	Ferrari
2001	Michael SCHUMACHER (GER)	Ferrari
2000	Michael SCHUMACHER (GER)	Ferrari
1999	Mika HAKKINEN (FIN)	Ferrari
1998	Mika HAKKINEN (FIN)	McLaren - Mercedes
1997	Jacques VILLENEUVE (CAN)	Williams - Renault
1996	Damon HILL (GBR)	Williams - Renault
1995	Michael SCHUMACHER (GER)	Benetton - Renault
1994	Michael SCHUMACHER (GER)	Williams - Renault
1993	Alain PROST (FRA)	Williams - Renault
1992	Nigel MANSELL (GBR)	Williams - Renault
1991	Ayrton SENNA (BRA)	McLaren - Honda
1990	Ayrton SENNA (BRA)	McLaren - Honda
1989	Alain PROST (FRA)	McLaren - Honda
1988	Ayrton SENNA (BRA)	McLaren - Honda
1987	Nelson PIQUET (BRA)	Williams - Honda
1986	Alain PROST (FRA)	Williams - Honda
1985	Alain PROST (FRA)	McLaren - TAG/Porsche
1984	Niki LAUDA (AUT)	McLaren - TAG/Porsche

1983	Nelson PIQUET (BRA)	Ferrari
1982	Keke ROSBERG (FIN)	Ferrari
1981	Nelson PIQUET (BRA)	Williams - Ford/Cosworth
1980	Alan JONES (AUS)	Williams - Ford/Cosworth
1979	Jody SCHECKTER (SAF)	Ferrari
1978	Mario ANDRETTI (USA)	Lotus - Ford/Cosworth
1977	Niki LAUDA (AUT)	Ferrari
1976	James HUNT (GBR)	Ferrari
1975	Niki LAUDA (AUT)	Ferrari
1974	Emerson FITTIPALDI (BRA)	McLaren - Ford/Cosworth
1973	Jackie STEWART (GBR)	Lotus - Ford/Cosworth
1972	Emerson FITTIPALDI (BRA)	Lotus - Ford/Cosworth
1971	Jackie STEWART (GBR)	Tyrrell - Ford/Cosworth
1970	Jochen RINDT (AUT)	Lotus - Ford/Cosworth
1969	Jackie STEWART (GBR)	Matra - Ford/Cosworth
1968	Graham HILL (GBR)	Lotus - Ford/Cosworth
1967	Denny HULME (NZL)	Brabham - Repco
1966	Jack BRABHAM (AUS)	Brabham - Repco
1965	Jim CLARK (GBR)	Lotus - Climax
1964	John SURTEES (GBR)	Ferrari
1963	Jim CLARK (GBR)	Lotus - Climax
1962	Graham HILL (GBR)	BRM
1961	Phil HILL (USA)	Ferrari
1960	Jack BRABHAM (AUS)	Cooper - Climax
1959	Jack BRABHAM (AUS)	Cooper - Climax
1958	Mike HAWTHORN (GBR)	Vanwall
1957	Juan Manuel FANGIO (ARG)	Independent
1956	Juan Manuel FANGIO (ARG)	Independent
1955	Juan Manuel FANGIO (ARG)	Independent
1954	Juan Manuel FANGIO (ARG)	Independent
1953	Alberto ASCARI (ITA)	Independent
1952	Alberto ASCARI (ITA)	Independent
1951	Juan Manuel FANGIO (ARG)	Independent
1950	Giuseppe 'Nino' FARINA (ITA)	Independent

QUIZANSWERS

FIND JENSON ANSWERS (PG 34)

SPOT THE DIFFERENCE ANSWERS (PG 16)
The differences are circled

SPOT THE DIFFERENCE ANSWERS (PG 49)
The differences are circled

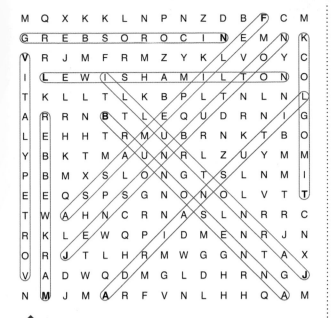

Wordsearch grid:

```
M Q X K K L N P N Z D B F C M
G R E B S O R O C I N E M N K
V R J M F R M Z Y K L V O Y C
I L E W I S H A M I L T O N O
T K L L T L K B P L T N L N L
A R R N B T L E Q U D R N I G
L E H H T R M U B R N K T B O
Y B K T M A U N R L Z U Y M M
P B M X S L O N G T S L N M I
E E Q S P S G N O N O L V T T
T W A H N C R N A S L N R R C
R K L E W Q P I D M E N R J N
O R J T L H R M W G G N T A X
V A D W Q D M G L D H R N G J
N M J M A R F V N L H H Q A M
```

▲ **WORDSEARCH SOLUTION (PG 33)**

Crossword Solution:

1. TIMOGLOCK
2. POLEPOSITION
6. LOLLIPOP
8. TYREWARMER
9. ITALIAN
11. STEWARD
12. CHICANE
14. YELLOWFLAG
17. CHAMPAGNE
18. WETTYRES

Down clues: TENPOINTS, KARUNCHANDHOK, SILVERSTONE, SAFETYCAR, INDIA, POLAND, PODIUM, HELMET, COCKPIT

▲ **CROSSWORD SOLUTION (PG 25)**

THE BIG F1 QUIZ
ANSWERS FROM (PG 40)

01, NICO HULKENBERG
02, MARK WEBBER
03, MICHAEL SCHUMACHER, NICO ROSBERG, ADRIAN SUTIL, TIMO GLOCK, NICO HULKENBERG
04, RACE MARSHAL
05, BRAWN-GP
06, RUSSIA
07, SEVEN
08, CANADIAN AND FRENCH GPS
09, BAHRAIN
10, JENSON BUTTON
11, BOTH HAVE STREET CIRCUITS
12, FELIPE MASSA
13, IT WAS THE 60TH ANNIVERSARY OF F1 GRAND PRIX
14, NICO ROSBERG
15, FERNANDO ALONSO
16, SECOND
17, TWO
18, FERRARI
19, SEBASTIAN VETTEL
20, B) 2006

WHICH CIRCUIT?
ANSWERS (PG 42)

A, MONACO
B, BAHRAIN
C, CANADA
D, VALENCIA, SPAIN

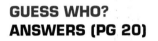

GUESS WHO?
ANSWERS (PG 20)

1, Mark Webber
2, Fernando Alonso
3, Sebastian Vettel
4, Jenson Button